The Amazing Things We Can See with A Telescope!
An Introduction to Astronomy

C. Chérie Hardy
Avant-garde Books, LLC

Avant-garde Books™

Avant-garde Books, LLC
Post Office Box 566
Mableton, Georgia 30126
www.avantgardebooks.net

The Amazing Things We Can See with A Telescope!
An Introduction to Astronomy

ISBN: 978-1-946753-52-6

Printed in the United States of America

For bulk purchases and discounts for nonprofit organizations, contact Avant-garde Books at avantgardebooks@gmail.com.

Connect with Avant-garde Books, LLC!

f   @avantgardebooks100

🐦   @Avant_GardeBks

📷   @avantgardebooks

This book is dedicated to my brilliant and beautiful student, Neomi Warwick.

Here is an empowering quote to keep in your heart, "The sky is not the limit if you're reaching for the stars."-Author Unknown

Hello. My name is Malcolm Hamilton. I love school and my favorite subject is science. I feel fortunate that I have wonderful people around me like my parents and grandparents who **reiterate** the importance of getting an education. They encourage me to do my best in school; they support me by getting things that help me explore my interests. Last summer, for my birthday, my grandparents bought me a **telescope** because I told them that I liked **astronomy,** the scientific study of the stars, planets, and other objects in outer space.

My grandfather often tells me I can become an **astronaut**, like Ronald McNair, or anything I want to be if I acquire the right information, work hard, **collaborate** well with my **peers**, and maintain good **character**.

After doing some **research**, I learned that astronauts are people who travel to outer space. In the United States, NASA (National Aeronautics and Space Administration) is responsible for training scientists to **observe** and **analyze** what they see when they go on space missions.

Pictured: (left) Dr. Mae Jemison (October 17, 1956), the first African American woman to travel to space and (right) Ronald McNair (October 21, 1950 – January 28, 1986) who was a **physicist** and NASA astronaut. McNair died with six other people when the Space Shuttle Challenger exploded shortly after launching from the Kennedy Space Center.

The spacecrafts that NASA designs are equipped with instruments that make sure astronauts stay safe. That is because when people leave Earth, they are not able to breathe without a protective space suit.

Humans need **oxygen** to breathe, and most of space is a **vacuum** which means there are no gases. However, a spacecraft has its own oxygen and **nitrogen** to provide astronauts with the air they need to stay alive.

Pictured: Astronaut and Atlantis Mission Specialist, Leland Melvin (2009)
Photo Credit: NASA

When astronauts leave Earth, they must bring food to stay healthy. However, they cannot consume too much salt. In space, astronauts suffer from bone loss. High quantities of salt would **exacerbate** this problem. Water is also essential for successful space missions. Astronauts have a special process for creating their own water on spaceships. They use the water that comes from the conversion of **hydrogen** to **electricity**. This water must be **conserved** and **recycled** as much as possible. I have included some websites in the back of this book if you want to know more details about surviving in outer space. There are many dangers that astronauts face, but prior to their travel, they spend thousands of hours training as well as studying the right things to ensure they have successful missions.

When people look in the sky, they can see just a small fraction of what is in outer space. However, telescopes enable scientists to observe objects and occurrences in outer space that people cannot see with their naked eyes. There are different kinds of telescopes. The one that I have gives me a limited view, but there are large, multi-million-dollar ones that are usually kept at **observatories** around the world. These amazing machines allow astronomers to see **galaxies**, stars, and planets that are far away from Earth.

The Hubble Space Telescope

Photo Credit: NASA

Some telescopes make "space-based" observations like the Hubble Space Telescope which was the world's first of its kind to be launched into space in 1990. It has made over one million observations. As it orbits around Earth, it takes pictures and transmits that information to scientists.

Fun Fact: Dr. Edwin Hubble was an **astronomer** who used research to confirm the existence of extra galaxies that were once thought to be clouds of dust and gas. NASA honored Dr. Hubble for his groundbreaking findings and named the world's first optical, space-based telescope after him.

According to astronomers, there are many different galaxies in space. Earth is in the Milky Way galaxy. Within each galaxy, there are various planetary systems. We live in a **solar** system which is named after our biggest star, the sun. Eight planets (Earth, Jupiter, Mars, Mercury, Neptune, Saturn, Uranus, and Venus); five dwarf planets (Pluto, Ceres, Eris, Makemake, and Haumea), over 200 moons, and over one million **asteroids** are connected in our galaxy by **gravity.**

Using powerful telescopes, NASA has discovered other systems with orbiting stars beyond the solar system within the Milky Way galaxy.

Oceans cover about 70% of Earth's surface. Antarctica is the coldest place on Earth. It takes approximately 365 days for Earth to travel around the sun. Earth is slightly tilted as it moves around the sun which makes our weather and seasons change. When Earth is tilting away from the sun, it is winter; it is summer when it is tilting toward the sun.

Earth

The Sun is a big and bright star that is 93 million miles away from Earth. It is almost five billion years old. The Sun moves fast; it travels 448,000 miles per hour. It is super hot; the Sun's surface temperature is 10,022 degrees Fahrenheit.

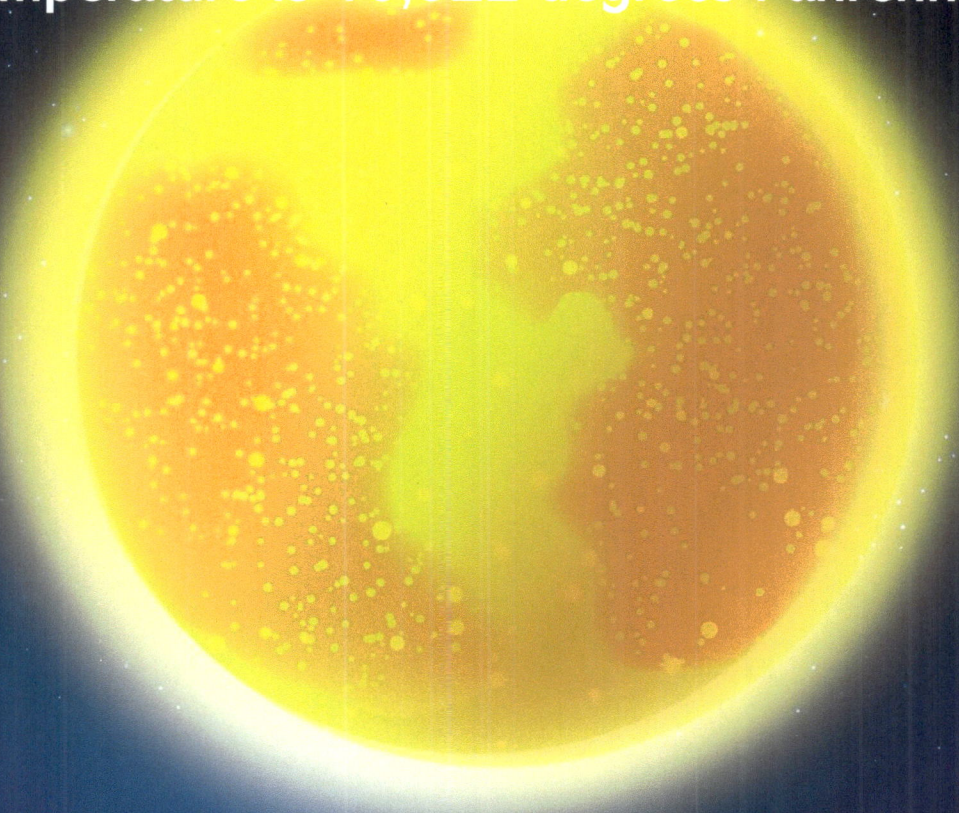

Sun

Jupiter is the largest planet in our solar system. The big red spot seen on Jupiter is actually a storm that scientists believe has been raging for over 300 years. Jupiter has bright-colored clouds and 79 moons.

Jupiter

Mars, also known as the "Red Planet", is a cold planet with poisonous and thin air. While it is the second smallest planet in our solar system, it is home to the tallest mountain. Scientists have discovered evidence of liquid water on the planet. On February 18, 2021, NASA's Perseverance rover landed on Mars to take pictures and search for signs of <u>microbial</u> life. A rover is robot that carries tools and cameras to help scientists see images in space.

Mars

Mercury is the smallest planet in our solar system. It is the closest to the sun, yet it is only the second hottest. Mercury has no air. 88 days would make up an entire year on the planet!

Mercury

Neptune is so far from Earth that it would take close to 165 Earth years to do a single lap around the sun. Neptune has 14 moons. In 1977, NASA sent a spacecraft to Neptune. It took 12 years for it to reach the planet!

Neptune

Saturn is one of the planets that can be seen with the naked eye. People cannot live there because it is mainly made up of hydrogen. The rings you see around the planet are made of large pieces of ice and rock. Titan is a giant moon on Saturn. It is bigger than Mercury!

Saturn

Uranus is the coldest planet in our solar system. It gets it blue color from poisonous gases. It spins on its side. In other words, instead of turning like a top, Uranus moves like a barrel.

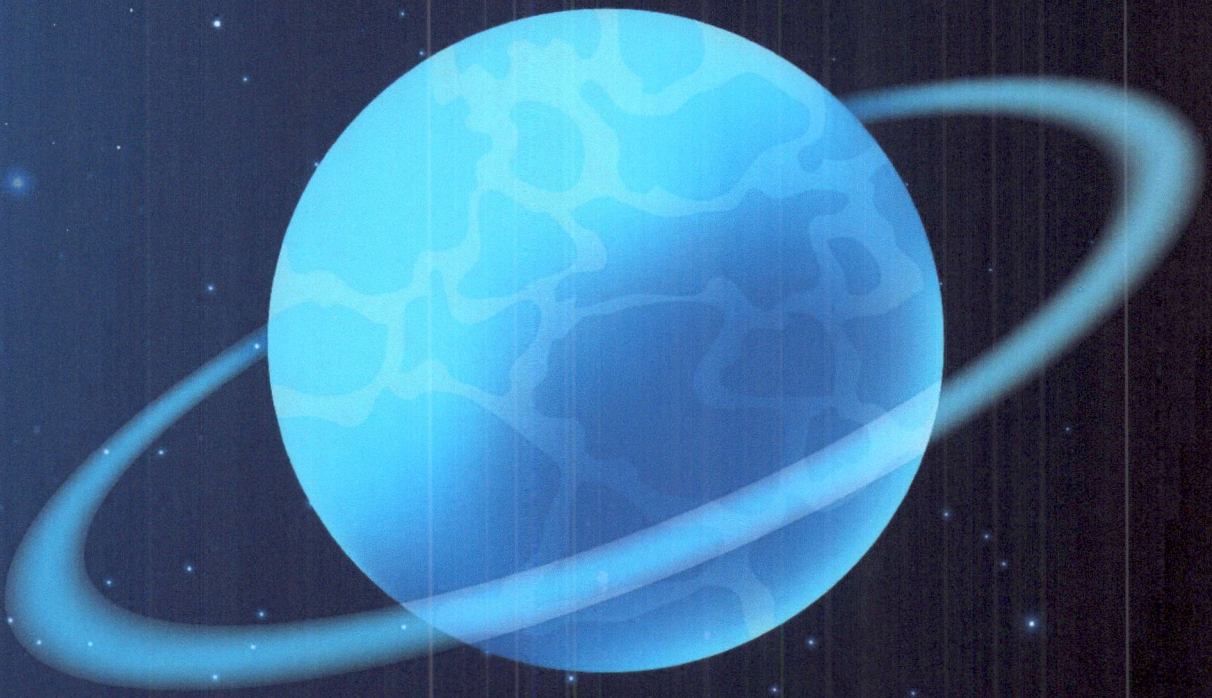

Uranus

Venus is one of Earth's closest neighbors. It spins backward. The poisonous gases around Venus hold the sun's rays and make it our solar system's hottest planet. In fact, the temperature on Venus is about 900°F.

Venus

Our planet has only one moon. There is no wind and no atmosphere there, yet there are <u>quakes</u>. The moon affects the rise and fall of ocean tides on Earth. Neil Armstrong became the first person to walk on the moon. He and two other astronauts, Michael Collins and Edwin "Buzz" Aldrin made history on July 20, 1969 when they took pictures and collected samples and rock and dirt from the moon's surface.

Moon

At one time, scientists considered Pluto a planet. However, today it is called a "dwarf planet" which means that it is much smaller than the other ones in our solar system. Dwarf planets often share their orbits with other space objects. They have either a egg or round shape. Pluto is round and has a variety of surface features including mountains and ice made of nitrogen and methane. Pluto is one of the coldest places in our solar system with temperatures about -375 degrees Fahrenheit.

Pluto

On the following pages, keep an observation log of the amazing things that you see with your telescope.

Observation Log

Date: _____

_____

_____

_____

_____

_____

_____

_____

Observation Log

Date: _____

_____

_____

_____

_____

_____

_____

_____

Observation Log

Date: _____

_____

_____

_____

_____

_____

_____

_____

Observation Log

Date: _____

_____

_____

_____

_____

_____

_____

_____

*Glossary

analyze (verb) - to study (something) closely and carefully: to learn the nature and relationship of the parts of (something) by a close and careful examination

asteroid (noun) - one of thousands of rocky objects that move in orbits mostly between those of Mars and Jupiter and have diameters from a fraction of a mile to nearly 500 miles

astronaut (noun) - a person who travels in a spacecraft into outer space

astronomer (noun) - a person who specializes in the scientific study of stars, planets, and other objects in outer space

astronomy (noun) - the scientific study of stars, planets, and other objects in outer space

character (noun) - moral excellence

collaborate (verb) - to work with another person or group in order to achieve or do something

conserve (noun) - to prevent the waste of; to keep in a safe condition

electricity (noun) - a form of energy that is carried through wires and is used to operate machines, lights, etc.

exacerbate (verb) - to make (a bad situation, a problem, etc.) worse

gravity (noun) - the natural force that tends to cause physical things to move towards each other; the force that causes things to fall towards the Earth

hydrogen (noun) - a chemical element that has no color or smell and that is the simplest, lightest, and most common element

microbial (adjective) - relating to an extremely small living thing that can only be seen with a microscope

nitrogen (noun) - a chemical that has no color or smell and that makes up a large part of the atmosphere

*Glossary

observatory (noun) - a special building for studying stars, planets, weather, etc.; a building from which scientists study and watch the sky

observe (verb) - to watch and sometimes also listen to (someone or something) carefully

oxygen (noun) - a chemical that is found in the air, that has no color, taste, or smell, and that is necessary for life

peer (noun) - a person who belongs to the same age group or social group as someone else

physicist (noun) – someone who specializes in the science that deals with matter and energy and the way they act on each other in heat, light, electricity, and sound

recycle (verb) - to send (used newspapers, bottles, cans, etc.) to a place where they are made into something new

reiterate (verb) - to repeat something you have already said in order to emphasize

research (noun or verb) - careful study that is done to find and report new knowledge about something; to carefully study a subject to find out information about it

scientist (noun) - a person who studies, specializes in, or investigates a field of science and does scientific work

solar (adjective) - of or relating to the sun

telescope (noun) - a device shaped like a long tube that you look through in order to see things that are far away

vacuum (noun) - an empty space in which there is no air or other gas : a space from which all or most of the air has been removed

*Taken from www.m-w.com

Activities

Activity A   Reading Comprehension

Directions: Complete each sentence with the correct answer based on what you read.

1. _____ is the scientific study of the stars, planets, and other objects in outer space.
2. There are _____ known dwarf planets in our solar system.
3. _____ is also called the "Red Planet".
4. A _____ allows people to see things far away, including what is in outer space.
5. _____ is the smallest planet in our solar system.
6. Earth moves around the _____.
7. _____ cover about 70% of Earth's surface.
8. The large red spot on Jupiter is actually a _____.
9. The force by which a planet or other celestial bodies are drawn toward its center is called_____.
10. _____ is the largest planet in our solar system.
11. Earth is a part of the _____ galaxy.
12. There are _____ planets in our solar system.
13. Within each galaxy, there are _____.
14. Humans need _____ to breathe which does not exist in outer space.
15. _____ are scientists who study astronomy and travel to outer space.
16. The rings around Saturn are made up of _____.
17. _____ was once considered the ninth planet in our solar system, but now scientists believe it is a dwarf planet.
18. An _____ is a place where people can see natural phenomena in outer space, usually with large telescopes.

Activities

Directions: Answer the following questions. Write your answers in the spaces below.

1.   What is the coldest planet in our solar system?

2.   Who was the first African-American woman to travel into outer space?

3.   What planet spins backwards?

4.   What planet has 14 moons?

5.   What organization is responsible for the United States' space program, including aeronautics and research?

6.   True or False. The moon has 100 miles per hour winds.

7.   True or False.   The sun is 1,000 degrees Fahrenheit.

1. _____
2. _____
3. _____
4. _____
5. _____
6. _____
7. _____

Activities

Vocabulary (Astronomy)

Directions: Find the words listed below in the wordsearch puzzle.

analyze	Mercury	asteroids	celestial
astronaut	moon	astronomer	Earth
galaxy	observatory	hydrogen	gravity
planet	rover	oxygen	NASA
Solar	Uranus	Mars	physicist
Sun	vacuum	Neptune	Saturn
Telescope	Venus	Pluto	star

```
A U R A N U S E D C M A N E S
G S X Z C B A N E A W S G P V
R G T H J R E L R S T T B O J
A M Z R T G E S Z U E E A C G
V T E H O S T U A N O R T S A
I M S R T N N M V E Q O W E O
T R D I C Z O U O V D I R L M
Y Y A V C U H M S O N D M E R
H L X L A I R J E E N S J T M
S N H A O C S Y G R E V O R T
A A Z N L S U Y A N A L Y Z E
T S G K N A X U H P L U T O N
U A M U Y O G T M P R A T S A
R I O B S E R V A T O R Y S L
N T W V B E N U T P E N Q T P
```

Activities

Directions: Find out more about the following African-American astronauts, mathematicians, and aeronautical engineers.

Notable African-American Astronauts

1. Michael P. Anderson (December 5, 1959 – February 1, 2003)
2. *Michael E. Belt (September 9, 1957)
3. Guion Bluford (November 22, 1942)
4. Charles Bolden (August 19, 1946)
5. *Yvonne Cagle (April 24, 1959)
6. Robert Curbeam (March 5, 1962)
7. Alvin Drew (November 5, 1962)
8. *Jeanette J. Epps (November 2, 1970)
9. Victor J. Glover (April 30, 1976)
10. Frederick D. Gregory (January 7, 1941)
11. Bernard A. Harris, Jr. (June 26, 1956)
12. Joan Higginbotham (August 3, 1964)
13. *Livingston L. Holder, Jr. (September 29, 1956)
14. Mae Jemison (October 17, 1956)
15. *Robert Henry Lawrence, Jr. (October 2, 1935 – December 8, 1967)
16. Ronald McNair (October 21, 1950 – January 28, 1986)
17. Leland D. Melvin (February 15, 1964)
18. **Arnaldo Tamayo Méndez (Cuban) (January 29, 1942)
19. Robert Satcher (September 22, 1965)
20. Winston E. Scott (August 6, 1950)
21. *Jessica Watkins (May 14, 1988)
22. Stephanie P. Wilson (September 27, 1966)

*Never traveled into space

** Afro-Latino

Notable African-American Mathematicians

1. Benjamin Banneker (November 9, 1731- October 9, 1806)
2. Augustin Banyaga (March 31, 1947)
3. Charles Bernard Bell, Jr. (August 20, 1928 – October 26, 2010)
4. David Blackwell (April 24, 1919 –July 8, 2010)
5. Marjorie Lee Browne (September 9, 1914 – October 19, 1979)
6. W. W. S. Claytor (January 4, 1908 – July 14, 1967)
7. Elbert Frank Cox (December 5, 1895 – November 28, 1969)
8. *Christine Darden (September 10, 1942)
9. *Annie Easley (April 23, 1933 – June 25, 2011)
10. Etta Zuber Falconer (November 21, 1933 – September 19, 2002)
11. *Evelyn Boyd Granville (May 1, 1924)
12. Euphemia Haynes (September 11, 1890 – July 25, 1980)
13. *Mary Jackson (April 9, 1921 – February 11, 2005)
14. *Katherine Johnson (August 26, 1918 – February 24, 2020)
15. William A. Massey (1956)
16. Kelly Miller (July 18, 1863 – December 29, 1939)
17. Charles Lewis Reason (July 21, 1818 – August 16, 1893)
18. Albert Turner Reid (November 13, 1927 – February 26, 1985)
19. Clarence Francis Stephens (July 24, 1917)
20. Lee Vernon Stiff (1949)
21. *Dorothy Vaughn (September 20, 1910 – November 10, 2008)
22. J. Ernest Wilkins, Jr. (November 27, 1923 – May 1, 2011)
23. Dudley Weldon Woodard (October 3, 1881 – July 1, 1965)

*Worked for NASA

Aeronautical Engineers

1. *Wanda M. Austin (1954)
2. Walter Braithwaite (January, 1945)
3. *April Ericsson (April 1, 1963)
4. William Fauntroy (February 6, 1933)
5. *Raye Montague (January 21, 1935 – October 9, 2018)
6. *Valerie Thomas (February 8, 1943)

Answers

Activity A

1. Astronomy
2. Five
3. Mars
4. Telescope
5. Mercury
6. Sun
7. Oceans
8. Storm
9. Gravity
10. Jupiter
11. Milky Way
12. eight
13. Planetary systems
14. oxygen
15. astronauts
16. Ice and rock
17. Pluto
18. observatory

Activity B

1. Neptune
2. Dr. Mae Jemison
3. Venus
4. Neptune
5. NASA
6. False
7. False

Answers

Activity C

```
A U R A N U S E D C M A N E S
G S X Z C B A N E A W S G P V
R G T H J R E L R S T T B O J
A M Z R T G E S Z U E E A C G
V T E H O S T U A N O R T S A
I M S R T N N M V E Q O W E O
T R D I C Z Q U O V D I R L M
Y Y A V C U H M S O N D M E R
H L X L A I R J E E N S J T M
S N H A O C S Y G R E V O R T
A A Z N L S U Y A N A L Y Z E
T S G K N A X U H P L U T O N
U A M U Y O G T M P R A T S A
R I O B S E R V A T O R Y S L
N T W V B E N U T P E N Q T P
```

Keep Exploring!

References

www.creanoso.com

www.nasa.gov

www.sciencenews.org

www.sciencing.com

www.space.com

Connect with Avant-garde Books, LLC!

Avant-garde Books™

Website

www.avantgardebooks.net

Facebook

@avantgardebooks100

Twitter

@Avant_GardeBks

Instagram

@avantgardebooks

Email:

avantgardebooks@gmail.com

THANK YOU for your purchase!

www.ingramcontent.com/pod-product-compliance
Lightning Source LLC
Chambersburg PA
CBHW041427090426

42741CB00002B/66